my POWER JOURNAL

UPS!DE DOWN BOOKS

First published in Great Britain 2021 by Trigger
Trigger is a trading style of Shaw Callaghan Ltd & Shaw Callaghan 23 USA, INC.
The Foundation Centre
Navigation House, 48 Millgate, Newark
Nottinghamshire NG24 4TS UK

www.triggerpublishing.com
Copyright © 2021 Trigger Publishing
Cover art by Rebecca Prinn

All rights reserved. No part of this publication may be reproduced, stored in a retrieval system, or transmitted in any form or by any means, electronic, mechanical, photocopying, recording or otherwise, without prior permission in writing from the publisher.

British Library Cataloguing in Publication Data
A CIP catalogue record for this book is available upon request
from the British Library

ISBN: 978-1-78956-211-8

Designed by Fusion Graphic Design
Printed and bound in the United Kingdom
Paper from responsible sources

Illustration credits:
@yuls2000, @kaewta, @rattanachomphoo, @doodlebarn, @barsrsind, @halimqd, @Sketchepedia, @halinarusakova, @arina_gladyisheva, @doodlebarn
Illustrations by rawpixel.com / Freepik

my POWER JOURNAL

UPS!DE DOWN BOOKS

HOW TO USE
MY POWER JOURNAL

You are **bold** ... you are **BRAVE** ... you are FIERCE! And you can do anything you dedicate your heart and mind to. Open *My Power Journal*, grab a pen and show yourself what you're made of.

At the top of each page, you'll find writing prompts that will push you to discover your inner strength. Doodles for colouring in, guided list-making, affirmations and inspirational quotes are sprinkled throughout like little gifts to make your spirit soar.

Go ahead: be bold and journal your power!

MY POWER JOURNAL

Today my superpower is _____ ...

MY **POWER** JOURNAL

I am powerful when I _____ ...

MY POWER JOURNAL

Today I feel strong because_____ ...

I am STRONG in body and mind!

MY POWER JOURNAL

Something great happened today.
It was _____ ...

MY POWER JOURNAL

Not every day turns out as I had planned.
Today was_____ because ...

MY **POWER** JOURNAL

I can become more powerful by _____ ...

5 THINGS THAT MADE ME WHO I AM TODAY:

1. _____

2. _____

3. _____

4. _____

5. _____

MY **POWER** JOURNAL

Today my superpower is _____ ...

MY **POWER** JOURNAL

I am powerful when I _____ ...

EXERCISE: LION'S BREATH

Try this breathing exercise to help bring out your inner lion ... ROAR!

1. Kneel on the ground and rest your bottom on top of your feet. You can either keep your ankles crossed or keep them parallel with feet touching – whichever is most comfortable for you!
2. Place your hands on your knees, straighten your arms and spread your fingers.
3. With eyes closed, take a long, deep breath through your nose.
4. Breathe out forcefully through your mouth and make a 'HA!' sound as you do. While you exhale, open your mouth wide, pop your eyes open and stick out your tongue.
5. Relax your face, close your eyes, and take another long, deep breath through your nose.
6. Repeat this cycle 4 to 5 times. During the exhale, try bringing your gaze up to the centre of your forehead or the tip of your nose.

MY POWER JOURNAL

Today I feel strong because_____ ...

MY POWER JOURNAL

Something great happened today.

It was _____ ...

MY POWER JOURNAL

Not every day turns out as I had planned.

Today was _____ because …

'The world itself is the will to power – and nothing else!
And you yourself are the will to power – and nothing else!'

– *Friedrich Nietzsche*

MY **POWER** JOURNAL

Today my superpower is _____ ...

MY POWER JOURNAL

I am powerful when I _____ ...

MY POWER JOURNAL

Today I feel strong because_____ ...

MY POWER JOURNAL

Something great happened today.
It was _____ ...

MY POWER JOURNAL

Not every day turns out as I had planned.
Today was _____ because …

'When life puts you in tough situations, don't say, "Why me?" Just say, "Try me."'

– Dwayne 'The Rock' Johnson

MY POWER JOURNAL

I can become more powerful by _____ ...

MY POWER JOURNAL

Today my superpower is _____ ...

MY **POWER** JOURNAL

I am powerful when I _____ ...

MY POWER JOURNAL

Today I feel strong because_____ ...

MY **POWER** JOURNAL

Something great happened today.
It was _____ ...

TOP 5 THINGS THAT BRING ME STRENGTH:

1 _____
_____
2 _____
_____
3 _____
_____
4 _____
_____
5 _____
_____

MY POWER JOURNAL

Not every day turns out as I had planned.
Today was_____because …

MY **POWER** JOURNAL

I can become more powerful by _____ ...

MY **POWER** JOURNAL

Today my superpower is _____ ...

MY POWER JOURNAL

I am powerful when I _____ ...

MY POWER JOURNAL

Today I feel strong because_____ ...

'The most common way people give up their power is by thinking they don't have any.'

– Alice Walker

MY **POWER** JOURNAL

Something great happened today.
It was _____ ...

MY POWER JOURNAL

Not every day turns out as I had planned.

Today was _____ because ...

MY **POWER** JOURNAL

I can become more powerful by ....

I have the POWER to think POSITIVELY!

MY POWER JOURNAL

Today my superpower is _____ ...

MY POWER JOURNAL

I am powerful when I _____ ...

MY POWER JOURNAL

Today I feel strong because_____ ...

'Mastering others is strength. Mastering yourself is true power.'

– Lao Tzu

MY POWER JOURNAL

Something great happened today.
It was _____ ...

MY POWER JOURNAL

Not every day turns out as I had planned.

Today was_____because ...

EXERCISE: BREATHE TO RESET YOUR DAY

Try this breathing exercise to help get yourself back on track.

- Sit comfortably in a quiet place.
- Take a deep inhale through your nose for 1 ... 2 ... 3 ... 4.
- Then exhale through your mouth for 4 ... 3 ... 2 ... 1.
- Focus on making the length of your inhalation the same as the length of your exhalation.
- Continue this breathing exercise for five minutes. This should help clear your mind of all other things so that when you're finished you can re-enter your day, refreshed!

MY POWER JOURNAL

I can become more powerful by _____ ...

MY POWER JOURNAL

Today my superpower is _____ ...

MY POWER JOURNAL

I am powerful when I _____ ...

5 PEOPLE WHO HELP BOOST ME:

1 _____

2 _____

3 _____

4 _____

5 _____

MY POWER JOURNAL

Today I feel strong because_____ ...

MY POWER JOURNAL

Something great happened today.

It was _____ ...

MY POWER JOURNAL

Not every day turns out as I had planned.
Today was _____ because …

MY POWER JOURNAL

I can become more powerful by _____ ...

MY POWER JOURNAL

Today my superpower is _____ ...

'Make the best use of what is in your power, and take the rest as it happens.'

– *Epictetus*

MY **POWER** JOURNAL

I am powerful when I _____ ...

MY POWER JOURNAL

Today I feel strong because_____ ...

I am **Beautiful** *inside & out!*

MY POWER JOURNAL

Something great happened today.

It was _____ ...

MY POWER JOURNAL

Not every day turns out as I had planned.

Today was_____because ...

MY POWER JOURNAL

I can become more powerful by _____ ...

THESE ARE MY 'HAPPY PLACES':

1 _____

2 _____

3 _____

4 _____

5 _____

MY POWER JOURNAL

Today my superpower is _____ ...

MY POWER JOURNAL

I am powerful when I _____ ...

MY POWER JOURNAL

Today I feel strong because_____ ...

MY **POWER** JOURNAL

Something great happened today.

It was _____ ...

MY POWER JOURNAL

Not every day turns out as I had planned.

Today was _____ because …

'Character is power.'

— Booker T. Washington

MY POWER JOURNAL

I can become more powerful by _____ ...

MY POWER JOURNAL

Today my superpower is _____ ...

MY **POWER** JOURNAL

I am powerful when I _____ ...

MY POWER JOURNAL

Today I feel strong because_____ ...

MY POWER JOURNAL

Something great happened today.
It was _____ ...

5 THINGS I WANT TO TELL THE UNIVERSE:

1 _____

2 _____

3 _____

4 _____

5 _____

MY POWER JOURNAL

Not every day turns out as I had planned.

Today was _____ because ...

MY POWER JOURNAL

I can become more powerful by_____ ...

MY **POWER** JOURNAL

Today my superpower is _____ ...

MY POWER JOURNAL

I am powerful when I _____ ...

MY POWER JOURNAL

Today I feel strong because_____ ...

'When the whole world is silent, even one voice becomes powerful.'

— *Malala Yousafzai*

MY POWER JOURNAL

Something great happened today.
It was _____ ...

MY **POWER** JOURNAL

Not every day turns out as I had planned.
Today was_____because ...

EXERCISE: POWER UP!

Try these things when you want to feel most powerful:

- Go for a power walk around your neighbourhood.
- Choose a mantra from this book and spend a minute saying it over and over to yourself.
- Spend 10 minutes in silent meditation, to reconnect with yourself.
- Boost someone who is in need. There is strength in helping others!
- Connect with people who make you feel good about yourself.
- Create something that makes you happy. It could be a drawing, a craft, a story ... something just for you.
- Get out into nature and soak up all the positivity from the fresh air.
- Turn on your favourite dance song, close the curtains, raise the volume, and dance like crazy!

MY POWER JOURNAL

I can become more powerful by _____ ...

MY POWER JOURNAL

Today my superpower is _____ ...

MY POWER JOURNAL

I am powerful when I _____ ...

5 NOTES FOR 'FUTURE ME':

1. _____

2. _____

3. _____

4. _____

5. _____

MY POWER JOURNAL

I can become more powerful by _____ ...

MY POWER JOURNAL

Something great happened today.
It was _____ ...

MY POWER JOURNAL

Not every day turns out as I had planned.

Today was_____ because ...

MY POWER JOURNAL

I can become more powerful by _____ ...

MY **POWER** JOURNAL

Today my superpower is _____ ...

'If you realized how powerful your thoughts are, you would never think a negative thought.'

– Peace Pilgrim

MY POWER JOURNAL

I am powerful when I _____ ...

MY POWER JOURNAL

Today I feel strong because _____ ...

MY **POWER** JOURNAL

Something great happened today.
It was _____ ...

MY POWER JOURNAL

Not every day turns out as I had planned.

Today was _____ because ...

MY POWER JOURNAL

I can become more powerful by _____ ...

5 NOTES FOR 'FUTURE ME':

1. _____

2. _____

3. _____

4. _____

5. _____

MY POWER JOURNAL

Today my superpower is _____ ...